contents

Please note that Australian cup and
spoon measurements are metric.
A conversion chart appears on page 62.

know your spuds

To ensure the best results for your favourite potato-based pleasure, it's important to choose a spud that's up to the task. So read on...

1. Pontiac potatoes can be successfully cooked by almost every method. They have pinky-red skin and white, waxy flesh.

2. Desiree potatoes are ideal for boiling, roasting, baking and mashing, but are not suitable for deep-frying. They have pink skin and waxy yellow or golden flesh.

3. Pink fir apple potatoes are elongated with rosy skin and waxy flesh; they are best boiled and in salads. If unavailable, substitute kipfler or tiny new potatoes.

4. Bintje potatoes have white, creamy skin and waxy, yellow flesh; they can be boiled, deep-fried, roasted or mashed. If unavailable, substitute spunta, sebago or pontiac potatoes.

5. Patrone potatoes are not suited to mashing, but are best when boiled, sautéed or baked; they have creamy skin and waxy yellow flesh. If unavailable, use tiny new, kipfler or pink-eye potatoes.

6. Nicola potatoes have cream skin and waxy yellow flesh; they are well suited to boiling and are a great addition to salads. If unavailable, use tiny new, kipfler or pink fir apple potatoes.

7. Tiny new potatoes are also known as chats; they're not a variety, but an early harvest, having a thin, pale skin. Tiny new potatoes are good steamed as well as roasted, and can be eaten hot or cold in salads. If unavailable, substitute kipfler, pink-eye or nicola potatoes.

8. Kipfler potatoes are long and oval in shape, and have golden skin and waxy, yellow flesh. They are best when boiled, sautéed or baked, and are ideal for use in salads. Substitute tiny new or pink fir apple potatoes, if unavailable.

9. Coliban potatoes are well suited to baking, mashing and steaming, but may disintegrate when boiling. They have smooth white skin and floury flesh.

10. Spunta potatoes have brown skin and golden flesh and, while well suited to roasting, deep-frying, baking and mashing, they may disintegrate when boiled. If unavailable, use sebago potatoes.

11. Sebago potatoes have creamy skin and white flesh; brilliant as a mashing potato, they can also be successfully boiled, baked or fried.

12. Pink-eye potatoes are small and round with off-white skin, deep, purple eyes and waxy, yellow flesh; they are best boiled, deep-fried or baked. If unavailable, use spunta or kipfler potatoes.

potato and
vegetable curry

40g ghee

1 medium brown onion (150g), chopped finely

2 cloves garlic, crushed

1 tablespoon grated fresh ginger

1 red thai chilli, seeded, chopped finely

2 teaspoons ground cumin

2 teaspoons ground coriander

1 teaspoon garam masala

1 teaspoon ground turmeric

*5 medium desiree potatoes (1kg),
peeled, chopped coarsely*

600g pumpkin, peeled, chopped coarsely

2 cups (500ml) vegetable stock

1 cup (250ml) coconut milk

200g green beans, trimmed, halved

100g baby spinach leaves, trimmed

Heat ghee in large saucepan; cook onion, garlic, ginger and chilli, stirring, until onion is soft. Add spices; cook, stirring, until fragrant. Add potato and pumpkin, stir to coat in spice mixture.
Stir in stock and coconut milk, bring to a boil; simmer, covered, about 20 minutes or until potato is almost tender. Stir in beans; simmer, covered, about 5 minutes or until beans are just tender. Remove pan from heat; stir in spinach.

SERVES 4
Per serving 24.8g fat; 1991kJ

chicken

and potato pies

3 medium coliban
potatoes (600g),
peeled, chopped
coarsely

$1/4$ cup (60ml) milk

1 tablespoon
vegetable oil

1 medium brown onion
(150g), chopped finely

1 clove garlic, crushed

1 small carrot (70g),
chopped finely

250g chicken mince

1 tablespoon
tomato paste

400g can tomatoes

1 cup (100g) chopped
cauliflower florets

1 tablespoon finely
chopped fresh
flat-leaf parsley

Boil, steam or microwave potato until tender;
drain. Mash potato in medium bowl with milk.
Meanwhile, heat oil in large frying pan; cook
onion, garlic and carrot, stirring, until onion is
soft. Add chicken; cook, stirring, until browned.
Add paste and undrained crushed tomatoes;
cook, uncovered, about 15 minutes or until
mixture has thickened slightly. Add cauliflower;
cook, covered, about 10 minutes or until
vegetables are just tender. Stir in parsley.
Preheat oven to moderately hot. Spoon mixture
into four oiled 1-cup (250ml) ovenproof dishes,
top with potato. Bake, uncovered, in moderately
hot oven about 30 minutes or until browned.

SERVES 4
Per serving 13.5g fat; 1236kJ

slow-roasted lamb

with lemon and potatoes

2kg leg of lamb

3 cloves garlic, quartered

6 sprigs fresh oregano, halved

salt, pepper

1 large lemon (180g)

5 medium sebago potatoes (1kg), peeled, quartered lengthways

1 teaspoon finely chopped fresh thyme

Preheat oven to slow. Make 12 small cuts in lamb. Press garlic and oregano into the cuts. Rub lamb all over with salt and pepper. Cut rind from lemon; cut rind into very thin strips. Squeeze juice from lemon; you will need 1/3 cup (80ml) juice for this recipe.
Place lamb, upside down, in large baking dish; pour over juice, top with rind. Bake, covered, in slow oven 2 hours. Turn the lamb over; brush with pan juices. Bake, covered, a further 30 minutes.
Add potatoes to dish; sprinkle with thyme. Bake, covered, a further 1 3/4 hours. Remove cover; bake a further 15 minutes. Stand, covered loosely, 10 minutes before serving.

SERVES 4
Per serving 22.6g fat; 2919kJ

beef nachos
baked potato

4 large pontiac potatoes (1.2kg)

1/2 cup (60g) coarsely grated cheddar cheese

1/4 cup (60g) sour cream

2 tablespoons fresh coriander leaves

beef mixture

2 teaspoons vegetable oil

250g minced beef

1 small brown onion (80g), chopped finely

1 teaspoon ground cumin

pinch chilli powder

1 cup (250ml) tomato pasta sauce

1/4 cup (50g) rinsed, drained, canned red kidney beans

guacamole

1 medium avocado (250g)

1/2 small tomato (65g), seeded, chopped finely

1 tablespoon finely chopped brown onion

1 tablespoon lemon juice

few drops Tabasco sauce

Preheat oven to moderately hot. Place unpeeled potatoes on oven tray, prick all over with skewer or fork; bake, uncovered, in moderately hot oven about 1 1/4 hours or until tender.

Trim tops from potatoes, scoop out potato flesh, leaving 1cm shell. Coarsely chop potato flesh; add half of the potato flesh to beef mixture, use remaining potato for another use.

Spoon beef mixture into potatoes, top with cheese; bake, uncovered, in moderately hot oven about 15 minutes or until hot. Serve potatoes topped with guacamole, sour cream and coriander.

Beef Mixture Heat oil in medium frying pan; cook beef, stirring, until browned. Add onion, cumin and chilli; cook, stirring, until onion is soft. Add pasta sauce and beans, bring to a boil; simmer, uncovered, until mixture is thick, cool.

Guacamole Mash avocado coarsely in small bowl; stir in remaining ingredients.

SERVES 4
Per serving 29.9g fat; 2429kJ

potatoes anna

4 large patrone potatoes (1.2kg), peeled

100g butter, melted

salt, pepper

Preheat oven to very hot. Cut potatoes into very thin slices, pat dry with absorbent paper. Brush butter generously over 23cm-round enamel-coated cast-iron pan or ovenproof pie plate. **Place** a layer of overlapping potato slices over base of prepared pan, brush with more of the butter, sprinkle with salt and pepper. Repeat layering until all slices are used, ending with butter. **Cover** with foil; bake in very hot oven 20 minutes. Remove foil; bake a further 30 minutes or until top is crisp and golden brown and potato is cooked through. Turn onto plate, cut into wedges to serve.

SERVES 4
Per serving
20.8g fat; 1584kJ

chicken and corn
croquettes

5 medium sebago potatoes (1kg), peeled, chopped coarsely

2 egg yolks

2 tablespoons cream

2 x 130g cans corn kernels, rinsed, drained

1½ cups (255g) finely chopped cooked chicken

¼ cup finely chopped fresh flat-leaf parsley

1 chicken stock cube

plain flour

2 eggs, beaten lightly

1½ cups (150g) packaged breadcrumbs

vegetable oil, for deep-frying

Boil, steam or microwave potato until tender; drain. Mash potato in large bowl until smooth; stir in egg yolks, cream, corn, chicken, parsley and crumbled stock cube. Cover; refrigerate 30 minutes

Shape ¼-cup amounts of mixture into croquette shapes. Coat croquettes in flour; shake off excess flour. Dip croquettes in egg; coat in breadcrumbs. Cover, refrigerate 30 minutes.

Heat oil in large saucepan; deep-fry croquettes, in batches, until browned, drain on absorbent paper.

SERVES 4
Per serving 62g fat; 4104kJ

12 warm potato, mushroom and broad **bean** salad

1kg tiny new potatoes, halved

400g button mushrooms, halved

100g mesclun

100g baby spinach leaves, trimmed

250g frozen broad beans, thawed, peeled

¼ cup (20g) parmesan cheese flakes

yogurt dressing

½ cup (140g) yogurt

2 teaspoons lemon juice

1 clove garlic, crushed

2 tablespoons seeded mustard

2 tablespoons milk

Preheat oven to very hot. Boil, steam or microwave potatoes until just tender. Transfer potatoes to large oiled baking dish; bake, uncovered, in very hot oven 10 minutes. Add mushrooms to dish; bake 5 minutes or until potatoes are browned and mushrooms are tender. Stand 5 minutes.

Combine potatoes, mushrooms, mesclun, spinach, beans, cheese and dressing in large bowl.

Yogurt Dressing Whisk ingredients in small bowl until smooth.

SERVES 4
Per serving
4.3g fat; 1162kJ

indian-spiced

lamb with aloo chop

¼ cup (70g) yogurt

¼ cup (75g) tandoori paste

¼ cup (60ml) lime juice

3 cloves garlic, crushed

1 tablespoon grated fresh ginger

1 tablespoon garam masala

3 (900g) lamb eye of loin

aloo chop

3 medium coliban potatoes (600g), peeled

30g butter

¾ cup (180g) sour cream

⅓ cup (50g) self-raising flour

½ teaspoon baking powder

Combine yogurt, paste, juice, garlic, ginger and garam masala in large bowl, add lamb. Cover; refrigerate 3 hours or overnight.
Remove lamb from marinade; discard marinade. Cook lamb, uncovered, on heated oiled grill plate (or grill or barbecue) until browned all over and cooked as desired. Serve lamb with aloo chop.
Aloo Chop Boil, steam or microwave potatoes until tender; drain. Mash potato, stir in remaining ingredients. Using hands, shape ¼-cup amounts of mixture into patties; cook in large heated oiled non-stick frying pan, in batches, until browned both sides.

SERVES 4
Per serving 36.3g fat; 2864kJ

warm chicken

and potato salad

1kg tiny new potatoes, halved

1 clove garlic, crushed

cooking-oil spray

4 bacon rashers, chopped coarsely

2½ cups (425g) coarsely chopped cooked chicken

½ cup (120g) light sour cream

¼ cup (75g) mayonnaise

¼ cup (60ml) buttermilk

2 tablespoons seeded mustard

¼ cup finely chopped fresh chives

Preheat oven to very hot. Combine potato and garlic in large baking dish; coat with cooking-oil spray. Bake, uncovered, in very hot oven about 30 minutes or until potatoes are brown and crisp. **Meanwhile**, cook bacon in medium heated frying pan until crisp; drain on absorbent paper. **Gently** toss potatoes, bacon and chicken in large bowl with combined cream, mayonnaise, buttermilk, mustard and chives.

SERVES 4
Per serving 31.3g fat; 2710kJ

smoked salmon and rosti stacks

200ml crème fraîche

1 tablespoon finely chopped fresh dill

2 tablespoons horseradish cream

1 teaspoon finely grated lemon rind

5 medium pontiac potatoes (1kg), peeled

1 clove garlic, crushed

1/2 teaspoon cracked black pepper

1/4 cup finely chopped fresh chives

1 egg, beaten lightly

1/4 cup (35g) plain flour

vegetable oil, for shallow-frying

16 thin slices (250g) smoked salmon

Combine crème fraîche, dill, horseradish cream and rind in small bowl.

Grate potatoes coarsely, squeeze out excess moisture. Combine potato in large bowl with garlic, pepper, chives, egg and flour; mix well.

Heat oil in medium frying pan; cook 1/4-cup amounts of potato mixture, in batches, until browned both sides and crisp. Drain on absorbent paper.

Place one rosti on each serving plate, top with two slices salmon and 1 tablespoon crème fraîche mixture; repeat, then finish each stack with a third rosti and remaining crème fraîche mixture.

SERVES 4
Per serving 52.3g fat; 3086kJ

18 garlic
kipfler potatoes

1kg kipfler potatoes
8 cloves garlic
1 teaspoon salt

Preheat oven to hot. Boil, steam or microwave unpeeled potatoes until just tender; drain. Cut potatoes in half lengthways; place in oiled baking dish with garlic; sprinkle with salt.
Bake, uncovered, in hot oven about 45 minutes or until potato is brown and crisp. Squeeze two of the garlic cloves over potato; shake gently to combine.

SERVES 4
Per serving 0.4g fat; 706kJ

potato omelette

1 tablespoon vegetable oil

1 large brown onion
(200g), sliced thinly

1 clove garlic, crushed

1small red capsicum
(150g), chopped finely

130g can corn
kernels, drained

2 teaspoons finely
chopped fresh oregano

2 medium spunta
potatoes (400g),
peeled, sliced thinly

6 eggs, beaten lightly

½ cup (125ml) thickened
cream

2 teaspoons finely chopped fresh thyme

½ cup (60g) finely grated cheddar cheese

Oil deep 19cm-square cake pan, line base and two opposite sides
with baking paper. Preheat oven to moderate.
Heat oil in small frying pan; cook onion, garlic and capsicum, stirring,
until onion is soft; drain, cool. Combine onion mixture with corn and
oregano. Layer half of the potato over base of prepared pan, top
with onion mixture, then remaining potato.
Pour combined eggs and cream over top; sprinkle with thyme and
cheese. Bake, uncovered, in moderate oven about 1 hour or until
potato is tender and top is browned lightly.

SERVES 4
Per serving 29.5g fat; 1829kJ

20 swordfish

with skordalia

4 swordfish
steaks (800g)

2 teaspoons olive oil

500g baby spinach
leaves, trimmed

1/3 cup (95g) yogurt

1 teaspoon finely
chopped fresh mint

2 teaspoons
lemon juice

skordalia

2 medium desiree
potatoes (400g),
peeled, chopped

6 cloves garlic,
crushed

2 slices stale
white bread

1/3 cup (80ml) olive oil

1 tablespoon
lemon juice

1 tablespoon white
wine vinegar

Cook fish in heated oiled grill pan (or grill or barbecue) until browned both sides and just cooked through.

Heat oil in same pan; cook spinach, stirring, until just wilted. Divide skordalia among serving plates; top with fish, spinach and combined yogurt, mint and juice.

Skordalia Boil, steam or microwave potato until tender; drain. Mash potato in medium bowl with garlic. Trim and discard crusts from bread; soak bread in small bowl of cold water. Drain and squeeze excess water from bread; add bread to potato mixture, beat until smooth. Gradually add combined oil, juice and vinegar; beat until smooth.

SERVES 4
Per serving 26g fat; 2069kJ

vichyssoise

60g butter

*1 large brown onion
(200g), chopped finely*

*2 medium leeks
(700g), sliced thinly*

*3 large bintje potatoes
(900g), peeled,
chopped coarsely*

*4 trimmed celery sticks
(300g),
chopped coarsely*

*2 litres (8 cups)
chicken stock*

³/₄ cup (180ml) cream

*2 tablespoons finely
chopped fresh chervil*

Heat butter in large saucepan; cook onion,
stirring, until soft. Add leek; cook, stirring,
about 10 minutes or until leek is soft.
Add potato and celery; cook, stirring,
2 minutes. Stir in stock, bring to a boil;
simmer, uncovered, about 15 minutes or
until potato is soft, stirring occasionally.
Blend or process soup, in batches, adding
cream gradually, until smoothly pureed.
Cover; refrigerate 3 hours or overnight.
Just before serving, sprinkle chervil
over cold soup.

SERVES 4
Per serving 34.7g fat; 2276kJ

sausages with
sweet onions and smash

1kg tiny new
potatoes, halved

1 tablespoon olive oil

3 medium red onions
(500g), sliced thickly

2 tablespoons red
wine vinegar

2 tablespoons
chicken stock

2 tablespoons
caster sugar

8 thick beef and
herb sausages

1/3 cup (80g)
sour cream

1 tablespoon finely
chopped fresh chives

Boil, steam or microwave potatoes until tender; drain.
Meanwhile, heat half of the oil in medium frying pan;
cook onion, stirring, until soft. Add vinegar, stock and
sugar; cook, stirring, until liquid is evaporated. Cook
sausages on heated oiled grill plate (or grill or barbecue)
until browned all over and cooked through.
Press potatoes with the back of a spoon. Divide potatoes
among serving plates, top with sour cream and chives;
serve with the sausages, topped with onion mixture.

SERVES 4
Per serving 54.7g fat; 3445kJ

24 rosti-topped sausages
with garlic cabbage

1kg thick beef sausages

1 medium brown onion (150g), chopped coarsely

1 clove garlic, crushed

400g can tomatoes

1 cup (250ml) water

2 tablespoons tomato paste

2 tablespoons finely chopped fresh flat-leaf parsley

1/2 teaspoon sweet paprika

rosti topping

5 medium spunta potatoes (1kg), peeled

1 cup (125g) coarsely grated cheddar cheese

garlic cabbage

30g butter

1/2 medium cabbage (750g), chopped coarsely

1 clove garlic, crushed

2 tablespoons dry white wine

2 tablespoons finely chopped fresh chives

Cook sausages in large heated frying pan, in batches, until browned all over. Drain on absorbent paper; slice thickly. Discard fat in pan; cook onion and garlic, stirring, until onion is soft. **Preheat** oven to moderately hot. Return sausages to pan with undrained crushed tomatoes, the water, paste and parsley, bring to a boil; simmer, uncovered, about 10 minutes or until mixture thickens. Place sausage mixture in shallow 3-litre (12 cup) ovenproof dish. Cover sausage mixture with rosti topping, sprinkle with paprika; bake, uncovered, in moderately hot oven about 30 minutes or until browned. Serve with garlic cabbage.

Rosti Topping Boil, steam or microwave potatoes until just tender; drain, cool. Coarsely grate potatoes into large bowl, combine with cheese.

Garlic Cabbage Heat butter in large saucepan; cook cabbage, garlic and wine, stirring, until cabbage is just tender. Just before serving, stir in chives.

SERVES 4
Per serving 81g fat; 4704kJ

cheesy potato
chicken

4 (680g) single
chicken breast fillets

5 medium desiree
potatoes (1kg), peeled

1 medium brown
onion (150g),
grated coarsely

1 cup (125g)
pizza cheese

2 tablespoons finely
chopped fresh chives

1 egg

cooking-oil spray

Using meat mallet, gently pound fillets between
sheets of plastic wrap until 1cm thick.
Boil whole potatoes until almost tender, cool
20 minutes; grate coarsely. Combine potato,
onion, cheese, chives and egg in large bowl.
Coat large frying pan with cooking-oil spray;
cook chicken until browned both sides and
tender. Top with potato mixture; cook under
hot grill until potato is browned.

SERVES 4
Per serving 12.4g fat; 2003kJ

potatoes
à la dauphinoise

4 large spunta potatoes (1.2kg), peeled, sliced thinly

pinch ground nutmeg

300ml cream

¼ cup (20g) finely grated parmesan cheese

20g butter

Preheat oven to moderate. Oil deep 19cm-square cake pan.

Layer potato in prepared pan, sprinkle with nutmeg. Pour over cream, sprinkle with cheese; dot with butter.

Bake, covered, in moderate oven 30 minutes, uncover; bake 45 minutes or until top is browned and potato is tender.

SERVES 4
Per serving 38.8g fat; 2337kJ

tandoori potato
and pumpkin pizza

1 cup (200g) yellow
split peas

1 litre (4 cups) water

2 tablespoons finely
chopped fresh coriander

400g pumpkin, peeled,
sliced thinly

4 medium pontiac potatoes
(800g), peeled, sliced thinly

2 teaspoons peanut oil

2 medium brown onions
(300g), sliced thinly

1 tablespoon grated
fresh ginger

2 x 26cm prepared
pizza bases

60g baby rocket leaves

1½ cups (420g) yogurt

2 tablespoons finely
chopped fresh mint

tandoori spice mix

2 teaspoons ground cumin

2 teaspoons
ground turmeric

2 teaspoons sweet paprika

2 teaspoons
ground coriander

¼ teaspoon cayenne pepper

2 teaspoons peanut oil

Rinse peas under cold water until water runs clear. Place peas and the water in medium saucepan, bring to a boil; simmer, uncovered, about 45 minutes or until tender, drain. Blend or process peas until smooth; transfer to medium bowl, stir in coriander.

Preheat oven to hot. Combine pumpkin, potato and tandoori spice mix in large baking dish. Bake, uncovered, in hot oven about 15 minutes or until just tender.

Meanwhile, heat oil in small saucepan; cook onion and ginger, stirring, until onion is soft. Place pizza bases on oven trays; spread with split pea mixture, top with onion and potato mixtures.

Bake, uncovered, in very hot oven about 15 minutes or until bases are crisp. Top pizzas with rocket, drizzle with combined yogurt and mint.

Tandoori Spice Mix Combine ingredients in small bowl.

SERVES 4
Per serving 17g fat; 4026kJ

traditional
irish stew

750g neck, rib or shoulder lamb chops

3 large brown onions (600g)

1 large carrot (180g)

1 large parsnip (180g)

5 medium pontiac potatoes (1kg)

salt, pepper

2½ cups (625ml) beef stock

1 teaspoon worcestershire sauce

1 tablespoon finely chopped fresh flat-leaf parsley

Remove any excess fat and sinew from lamb. Peel and slice onions, carrot, parsnip and potatoes into 1cm thick rounds.

Preheat oven to moderately slow. Layer the lamb, onion, carrot, parsnip and potato in large flameproof dish or pan, sprinkling lightly with salt and pepper on each layer. Pour in the stock and sauce; bring to a boil over high heat. Transfer dish to oven.

Bake, covered, in moderately slow oven about 3 hours or until meat is very tender and most of the liquid has been absorbed. For a browned top, remove the lid for the last 30 minutes of cooking. Serve sprinkled with parsley.

SERVES 4
Per serving 11.6g fat; 2010kJ

salmon patties

with lemon mayonnaise

3 medium sebago
potatoes (600g),
peeled, chopped
coarsely

1 tablespoon
vegetable oil

1 medium brown onion
(150g), chopped finely

2 cloves garlic, crushed

415g can pink salmon,
drained, flaked

2 teaspoons finely
grated lemon rind

2 tablespoons
coarsely chopped
fresh flat-leaf parsley

1 egg, beaten lightly

1/4 cup (35g) plain flour

1 egg, beaten
lightly, extra

1/2 cup (50g) packaged
breadcrumbs

vegetable oil,
for shallow-frying, extra

lemon mayonnaise

1/2 cup (150g)
mayonnaise

2 teaspoons
finely grated
lemon rind

Boil, steam or microwave potato until tender,
drain; mash coarsely. Heat oil in medium frying
pan; cook onion and garlic, stirring, until onion
is soft. Combine onion mixture, potato, salmon,
rind, parsley and egg in medium bowl. Using
hands, shape mixture into eight patties, place
on tray; refrigerate 30 minutes.
Coat patties in flour; shake off excess flour.
Dip patties in extra egg; coat in breadcrumbs.
Heat extra oil in large frying pan; shallow-fry
patties until browned both sides and heated
through, drain on absorbent paper. Serve
salmon patties with lemon mayonnaise.
Lemon Mayonnaise Combine ingredients
in small bowl.

SERVES 4
Per serving 58.1g fat; 3399kJ

32 not-so-humble mash

*We all know how rich and comforting mashed potatoes can be,
but who knew that mash could also be a creamy fusion of
flavours to complement any meal?*

creamy garlic mash

*5 medium sebago
potatoes (1kg), peeled,
chopped coarsely*

3 cups (750ml) milk

1 clove garlic, peeled

*40g butter,
chopped coarsely*

Place potato, milk and garlic
in medium saucepan, bring
to a boil; simmer gently, partially
covered, about 15 minutes or
until potato is soft. Discard garlic.
Strain potato over jug; reserve
½ cup (125ml) of the milk.
Transfer potato to large bowl; mash
with reserved milk and
butter until smooth.

bacon and parmesan mash

*5 medium sebago
potatoes (1kg), peeled,
chopped coarsely*

*4 bacon rashers,
chopped finely*

⅓ cup (80ml) buttermilk

*50g butter,
chopped finely*

*¼ cup (20g) finely grated
parmesan cheese*

*1 tablespoon finely
chopped fresh chives*

Boil, steam or microwave
potato until tender; drain.
Meanwhile, cook bacon in
large heated frying pan, stirring,
until crisp; drain on absorbent
paper. Transfer potato to
large bowl; mash with milk
and butter until smooth. Stir
in bacon, cheese and chives.

SERVES 4
Per serving 15.8g fat; 1516kJ

SERVES 4
Per serving 15.1g fat; 1505kJ

creamy garlic mash

bacon and parmesan mash

mustard and sweet onion mash

mustard and sweet onion mash

5 medium sebago potatoes (1kg), peeled, chopped coarsely

1 tablespoon olive oil

20g butter

2 large brown onions (400g), sliced thinly

2 teaspoons brown sugar

2 teaspoons balsamic vinegar

½ cup (125ml) hot milk

60g butter, chopped coarsely, extra

1 tablespoon dijon mustard

Boil, steam or microwave potato until tender; drain. **Meanwhile**, heat oil and butter in large frying pan; cook onion, stirring, until onion is soft and browned. Add sugar and vinegar; cook, stirring, until sugar dissolves. **Transfer** potato to large bowl; mash with milk, extra butter and mustard until smooth. Stir in half of the onion mixture; serve topped with remaining onion mixture.

SERVES 4
Per serving 22.6g fat; 1717kJ

34 coriander gnocchi
with roast tomato sauce

4 large nicola potatoes
(1.2kg), peeled,
chopped coarsely

1 egg

1 egg yolk

1½ cups finely
chopped fresh
coriander

1 teaspoon salt

1 clove garlic, crushed

1½ cups (225g)
plain flour

1¼ cups (100g)
finely grated parmesan
cheese

roast tomato sauce

700g cherry tomatoes

2 teaspoons coarsely
ground black pepper

2 tablespoons olive oil

1 medium brown onion
(150g), chopped finely

½ cup (125ml) dry
white wine

300ml thickened cream

Boil, steam or microwave potato until tender; drain. Mash potato in large bowl until smooth. Stir in egg, egg yolk, coriander, salt and garlic; using one hand, mix in flour. Knead potato mixture on floured surface, about 2 minutes or until smooth. Roll tablespoons of potato mixture into gnocchi-shaped ovals.

Add gnocchi to large saucepan of boiling water; cook, uncovered, about 3 minutes or until gnocchi float to surface. Remove gnocchi from pan with slotted spoon, place in bowl of iced water until cool; drain. Place gnocchi, in a single layer, on tray; cover, refrigerate.

Preheat oven to moderate. Place gnocchi in oiled shallow 2.5-litre (10 cup) ovenproof dish. Pour roast tomato sauce over top; sprinkle with cheese. Bake, uncovered, in moderate oven about 25 minutes or until cheese is browned lightly and gnocchi are hot.

Roast Tomato Sauce Combine tomatoes, pepper and half of the oil in medium baking dish. Bake, uncovered, in moderately hot oven about 10 minutes or until tomatoes are tender. Meanwhile, heat remaining oil in small saucepan; cook onion, stirring, until soft. Add wine; cook, stirring, until wine is reduced by half. Stir in cream and tomato; simmer, stirring, until sauce thickens slightly.

SERVES 4
Per serving 48.9g fat; 3926kJ

36

crunchy potatoes
bengali-style

1.5kg spunta potatoes, chopped coarsely

20g ghee

1 tablespoon panch phora

3 cloves garlic, crushed

1 tablespoon grated fresh ginger

1 red thai chilli, chopped finely

1 tablespoon ground cumin

60g ghee, extra

1 teaspoon salt

1 teaspoon cracked black pepper

1/4 cup (60ml) lemon juice

1/4 cup finely chopped fresh coriander

Boil, steam or microwave potato until almost tender; drain.

Heat ghee in small frying pan; cook panch phora, stirring, until fragrant. Add garlic, ginger, chilli and cumin; cook, stirring, 1 minute. Remove from heat.

Heat half of the extra ghee in large frying pan; add half of the potato, stir gently about 5 minutes or until browned and crisp. Remove from pan; repeat with remaining ghee and potato.

Return potato, with spice mixture, salt, pepper and juice, to pan; stir until just heated through. Just before serving, sprinkle with coriander.

SERVES 4
Per serving 18.3g fat; 1740kJ

potato
fattoush

1.5kg desiree
potatoes

2 large pieces
pitta bread

2 cups tightly
packed fresh
flat-leaf parsley,
chopped coarsely

1 medium brown
onion (150g),
sliced thinly

4 large egg
tomatoes (360g),
chopped coarsely

2 lebanese
cucumbers (260g),
sliced thinly

1/4 cup coarsely
chopped fresh mint

2/3 cup (160ml)
light olive oil

1/2 cup (125ml)
lemon juice

1/2 teaspoon
freshly ground
black pepper

Preheat oven to hot. Boil, steam or microwave
unpeeled whole potatoes until just tender; drain.
When cool enough to handle, peel potatoes;
cut into 2cm pieces.

Split each pitta in half; toast in hot oven until
crisp. Break pitta into small, even-sized pieces.
Combine pitta pieces with potato, parsley, onion,
tomato and cucumber in large bowl.

Just before serving, pour combined remaining
ingredients over fattoush mixture; toss gently
to combine.

SERVES 4
Per serving 38g fat; 3002kJ

seafood

potato pie

1 tablespoon olive oil

500g medium uncooked prawns, shelled

500g firm white fish fillets, chopped coarsely

200g scallops

60g butter

1 medium leek (350g), sliced thinly

1 clove garlic, crushed

1/4 cup (35g) plain flour

2 cups (500ml) milk

1/2 cup (60g) finely grated cheddar cheese

2 tablespoons finely chopped fresh flat-leaf parsley

1 tablespoon finely chopped fresh chives

potato topping

4 medium desiree potatoes (800g), peeled, chopped coarsely

40g butter, chopped coarsely

1/4 cup (60ml) buttermilk

1 tablespoon finely chopped fresh flat-leaf parsley

Heat oil in large frying pan; cook seafood, in batches, until cooked through. Place seafood into 5cm-deep, 2-litre (8 cup) ovenproof dish. Preheat oven to moderate. **Heat** butter in medium saucepan; cook leek and garlic, stirring, until leek is soft. Add flour; cook, stirring, until mixture thickens and bubbles. Gradually stir in milk; stir until mixture boils and thickens. Stir in cheese, parsley and chives. Drain any liquid from seafood in dish, then pour sauce over seafood. Place spoonfuls of potato topping over seafood mixture in dish. **Bake**, uncovered, in moderate oven about 25 minutes or until browned lightly and hot. **Potato Topping** Boil, steam or microwave potato until tender, drain; push potato through sieve into large bowl. Stir in remaining ingredients.

SERVES 4
Per serving 39.3g fat; 3191kJ

40 indian-style lamb and
potato skewers with yogurt sauce

12 tiny new potatoes
(480g), quartered

600g lamb fillets

$^1/_3$ cup (100g)
tikka paste

$^1/_4$ cup (70g) yogurt

1 small brown onion
(80g), grated coarsely

1 tablespoon finely
chopped fresh mint

yogurt sauce

1 cup (280g) yogurt

1 lebanese cucumber
(130g), seeded,
chopped finely

1 tablespoon finely
chopped fresh mint

1 tablespoon finely
chopped fresh chives

Boil, steam or microwave potato until almost
tender; drain. Cut lamb into 3cm pieces.
Thread lamb and potatoes onto 12 skewers.
Place skewers in large shallow dish; rub with
combined remaining ingredients.
Cook skewers on heated oiled grill plate (or grill
or barbecue) until browned all over and cooked
as desired. Serve skewers with yogurt sauce.
Yogurt Sauce Combine ingredients in small bowl.

SERVES 4
Per serving 16.4g fat; 1706kJ

baked potato
mornay

4 large pontiac
potatoes (1.2kg)

filling

125g asparagus,
chopped coarsely

20g butter

1 tablespoon
plain flour

¾ cup (180ml) milk

⅓ cup (40g) finely
grated cheddar cheese

3 green onions,
chopped finely

100g can salmon,
drained

Preheat oven to moderately hot. Pierce potato skins in several places with a skewer or fork. Place potatoes on oven tray; bake, uncovered, in moderately hot oven 1 hour or until tender. **Cut** tops from potatoes; scoop out flesh, leaving skins intact.

Combine coarsely chopped potato flesh with filling; divide mixture among potato shells. Bake potatoes, uncovered, in moderately hot oven about 15 minutes or until browned lightly. **Filling** Boil, steam or microwave asparagus until just tender; drain. Heat butter in medium

saucepan, add flour; cook, stirring, until mixture thickens and bubbles. Gradually stir in milk; stir until mixture boils and thickens. Remove pan from heat; stir in cheese, onion, salmon and asparagus.

SERVES 4
Per serving
12.2g fat; 1511kJ

42 spicy
cajun wedges
with dips

8 medium sebago
potatoes (1.6kg)

2 teaspoons
ground cumin

2 teaspoons
ground coriander

1 teaspoon
sweet paprika

1 teaspoon turmeric

1/2 teaspoon
ground oregano

pinch ground
chilli powder

2 tablespoons
olive oil

creamy chilli dip

125g packaged cream
cheese, softened

1/4 cup (60ml) sweet
chilli sauce

avocado dip

1 bacon rasher,
chopped finely

1 medium avocado (250g)

1 tablespoon finely
chopped fresh chives

tomato coriander salsa

2 small tomatoes (260g),
seeded, chopped finely

1 tablespoon finely
chopped red onion

1 tablespoon finely
chopped fresh coriander

SERVES 4
Per serving:
with creamy chilli dip 20.6g fat; 1973kJ
with avocado dip 20.4g fat; 1920kJ
with tomato coriander salsa 9.9g fat; 1504kJ

Preheat oven to very hot. Cut each potato in half; cut each half into four wedges. Combine wedges with remaining ingredients in large bowl.

Place wedges onto two oiled oven trays. Bake, uncovered, in very hot oven, about 50 minutes or until browned and crisp, swapping position of trays halfway through cooking. Turn wedges occasionally during cooking. Serve wedges with dips.

Creamy Chilli Dip Beat cream cheese and sauce in small bowl until smooth.

Avocado Dip Cook bacon in heated small frying pan, stirring, until crisp. Mash avocado in small bowl; stir in bacon and chives.

Tomato Coriander Salsa Combine ingredients in small bowl.

kipfler potato cakes

1kg kipfler potatoes, peeled

1 clove garlic, crushed

1 teaspoon lemon pepper seasoning

1/2 cup (60g) finely grated cheddar cheese

2 tablespoons sour cream

Boil, steam or microwave potatoes until just tender; drain. Mash potato; combine with remaining ingredients in large bowl, cool. Using hands, shape 1/3-cup amounts of mixture into patties. Cook patties, in batches, in large heated oiled frying pan until browned both sides and heated through.

SERVES 4
Per serving 9.2g fat; 1094kJ

crunchy baked **rosti**

*2 medium spunta
potatoes (400g), peeled*

1 teaspoon butter

1 medium leek (350g), sliced thinly

2 cloves garlic, crushed

1/2 teaspoon sweet paprika

*1/4 cup (20g) finely grated
parmesan cheese*

Preheat oven to very hot. Boil,
steam or microwave potatoes
until just tender; drain, cool.
Coarsely grate potato.
Melt butter in large frying
pan; cook leek, garlic and
paprika, stirring, until leek
is browned lightly.
Combine leek mixture, potato
and cheese in medium bowl.
Place 7.5cm egg ring on baking-
paper-lined oven tray, press
1/4 cup of potato mixture into ring;
gently remove ring. Repeat with
remaining potato mixture.
Bake rosti, uncovered, in very
hot oven about 20 minutes
or until browned.

SERVES 4
Per serving 2.8g fat; 463kJ

potato beef

lasagne

4 medium desiree potatoes (800g), peeled, sliced thinly

1 tablespoon olive oil

750g minced beef

1 medium brown onion (150g), chopped finely

2 cloves garlic, crushed

100g mushrooms, chopped finely

1 small carrot (70g), chopped finely

600g bottle tomato pasta sauce

2 tablespoons finely chopped fresh basil

1 cup (80g) finely grated parmesan cheese

cheese sauce

30g butter

2 tablespoons plain flour

2 cups (500ml) milk

1 cup (80g) finely grated parmesan cheese

1 teaspoon dijon mustard

Boil, steam or microwave potato until tender; drain.

Heat oil in large frying pan; cook beef, stirring, until browned. Add onion, garlic, mushrooms and carrot; cook, stirring, until onion is soft. Add pasta sauce and basil, bring to a boil; simmer, uncovered, about 5 minutes or until thick.

Preheat oven to moderate. Layer a third of the potato slices in oiled 3-litre (12 cup) shallow ovenproof dish; top with half of the beef mixture, then drizzle with a quarter of the cheese sauce. Repeat layering, then top with remaining potato slices and remaining cheese sauce; sprinkle with cheese. Bake, uncovered, in moderate oven about 30 minutes or until hot and browned. Stand 10 minutes before serving.

Cheese Sauce Heat butter in medium saucepan, add flour; cook, stirring, until mixture thickens and bubbles. Gradually stir in milk; stir until sauce boils and thickens. Remove pan from heat; stir in cheese and mustard.

SERVES 6
Per serving 31.5g fat; 2499kJ

potatoes with raclette
cheese and garlic

12 medium kipfler potatoes (1.5kg)

1 bulb garlic (70g)

40g butter

1 cup (125g) coarsely grated raclette cheese

Preheat oven to moderate. Wrap potatoes and whole garlic individually in foil. Place in baking dish. Bake in moderate oven about 30 minutes or until garlic is tender; remove garlic. Cook potatoes another 10 minutes or until tender. Cut garlic in half; squeeze out pulp into small bowl, stir in butter. **Partially** unwrap potatoes; cut lengthways down centre, not cutting all the way through potato or foil. Open out potatoes, cut foil around them. Divide butter mixture among potatoes; top with cheese. Cook potatoes under hot grill until cheese melts and bubbles. Serve with ocean trout, if desired.

SERVES 4

Per serving 18.5g fat; 1878kJ

german hot
potato salad

4 eggs

4 bacon rashers, chopped coarsely

750g tiny new potatoes

2 pickled gherkins, chopped finely

1 tablespoon finely chopped fresh flat-leaf parsley

²/₃ cup (200g) mayonnaise

¹/₃ cup (80g) sour cream

2 teaspoons lemon juice

Cover eggs with water in medium saucepan; bring to a boil. Simmer, uncovered, 10 minutes; drain. Cool eggs under cold water; shell and halve.
Meanwhile, cook bacon in medium heated frying pan until browned and crisp; drain on absorbent paper.
Boil, steam or microwave potatoes until tender; drain and halve. Combine remaining ingredients in same frying pan; stir over low heat until just hot. Place mayonnaise mixture in large bowl with potato, bacon and egg; toss gently to combine.

SERVES 4
Per serving 31g fat; 2106kJ

50 italian-style chicken
with potatoes
and broad beans

1kg tiny new
potatoes, halved

100g thinly sliced
spicy salami,
chopped finely

1kg chicken thigh
fillets, halved

250g frozen broad
beans, thawed, peeled

400g can tomatoes

1/4 cup (60ml)
dry red wine

2 tablespoons
tomato paste

1 teaspoon sugar

4 cloves garlic,
crushed

1 tablespoon finely
chopped fresh sage

2 tablespoons finely
chopped fresh
flat-leaf parsley

1/2 cup (40g)
finely grated parmesan
cheese

Boil, steam or microwave
potato until just tender; drain.
Cook salami in large heated
oiled frying pan until crisp;
remove from pan using a
slotted spoon. Cook chicken
in same pan until cooked
through and browned.
Preheat oven to moderate.
Place chicken and potato
in 2-litre (8 cup) shallow
ovenproof dish; top with
salami and beans.
Bring undrained crushed
tomatoes, wine, paste, sugar,
garlic, sage and parsley to
a boil in same frying pan.
Pour tomato sauce over
chicken and potato in dish,
top with cheese; bake,
uncovered, in moderate oven
40 minutes or until chicken
and potato are very tender
and cheese has browned.

SERVES 4
Per serving 31.3g fat; 3042kJ

spicy potato salad

25 tiny new potatoes (1kg)

1 teaspoon black mustard seeds

1 teaspoon ground cumin

1 teaspoon cumin seeds

1 clove garlic, crushed

2 tablespoons lemon juice

1/4 cup finely chopped fresh coriander

Boil, steam or microwave potatoes until just tender, rinse under cold water; drain, cool. **Heat** dry large frying pan, add spices; cook, stirring, until fragrant. Combine potatoes, spices and remaining ingredients in bowl; mix well.

SERVES 6
Per serving
0.3g fat; 475kJ

caramelised onion and potato frittata

1/4 cup (60ml) olive oil

2 medium brown onions (300g), sliced thinly

1 tablespoon brown sugar

1 tablespoon balsamic vinegar

5 medium sebago potatoes (1kg), peeled, sliced thinly

8 eggs

1/2 teaspoon sweet paprika

1 tablespoon finely chopped fresh flat-leaf parsley

2 cloves garlic, crushed

Heat 1 tablespoon of the oil in medium frying pan; cook onion, stirring, about 5 minutes or until soft and browned lightly. Add sugar and vinegar; cook, stirring, until caramelised.

Boil or steam potato until tender; drain. **Place** remaining oil in 22cm non-stick frying pan, arrange half of the potato over base, top with half of the onions; repeat. Cook, uncovered, over low heat, 5 minutes. **Whisk** together remaining ingredients in large jug, pour over potato in pan; cook over low heat until base of frittata is browned. Place pan under hot grill; cook until top is browned and frittata is set.

SERVES 4
Per serving
24.6g fat; 1968kJ

2 teaspoons olive oil

1 small brown onion (80g), chopped finely

1 small tomato (130g), chopped finely

2 tablespoons tomato paste

pinch chilli flakes

2 tablespoons coarsely grated cheddar cheese

3/4 cup (50g) stale breadcrumbs

8 chicken drumsticks (1.2kg)

1 clove garlic, crushed

potato-spinach bake

250g spinach, trimmed

4 medium spunta potatoes (800g), sliced thinly

1 cup (250ml) cream

2 cloves garlic, crushed

2 tablespoons seeded mustard

Heat half of the oil in small non-stick frying pan; cook onion, stirring, until soft. Add tomato, paste and chilli; cook, stirring, about 5 minutes or until liquid has evaporated. Stir in cheese and breadcrumbs.

Preheat oven to moderate. Loosen skin on drumsticks by sliding fingers between skin and meat. Gently push 1 tablespoon cooled tomato mixture under skin of each drumstick, secure with toothpicks; place on oven tray. Brush drumsticks all over with combined remaining oil and garlic.

Bake, uncovered, in moderate oven about 40 minutes or until drumsticks are browned and cooked through. Serve drumsticks with potato-spinach bake.

Potato-Spinach Bake Boil, steam or microwave spinach until just wilted; drain. Squeeze out excess liquid from spinach; chop finely. Layer a third of potato over base of oiled deep 19cm-square cake pan. Sprinkle with half the spinach; pour over a third of combined cream, garlic and mustard. Repeat layering, then top with remaining potato and cream mixture. Cover with foil; bake in moderate oven for 1 hour. Remove foil; bake about 30 minutes or until tender and browned lightly. Stand 10 minutes before serving.

SERVES 4
Per serving 53.5g fat; 3444kJ

crunchy potatoes with
fetta, spinach and bacon

1kg tiny new potatoes, halved

60g butter, melted

1 tablespoon olive oil

2 cloves garlic, crushed

1 teaspoon cracked black pepper

4 bacon rashers, chopped coarsely

2 tablespoons finely chopped fresh basil

½ cup (80g) kalamata olives

200g fetta cheese, chopped coarsely

100g baby spinach leaves

Preheat oven to very hot. Combine potatoes in large baking dish with butter, oil, garlic and pepper; bake, uncovered, in very hot oven about 30 minutes or until potatoes are browned, crisp and tender, turning potatoes occasionally during cooking.

Meanwhile, cook bacon in large heated frying pan, stirring, until crisp. Combine potatoes in large bowl with bacon, basil, olives, cheese and spinach, toss gently until combined.

SERVES 4
Per serving 31.6g fat; 2285kJ

kumara and potatoes
in peanut coconut sauce

2 medium
kumara (800g)

1 tablespoon peanut oil

2 medium brown onions
(300g), sliced thinly

2 cloves garlic, crushed

1 teaspoon grated
fresh ginger

1/2 teaspoon
sambal oelek

1 tablespoon mild
curry powder

1 teaspoon
ground cumin

1 teaspoon
ground coriander

1 tablespoon soy sauce

1/2 cup (140g) smooth
peanut butter

2 1/2 cups (625ml)
vegetable stock

1 cup (250ml)
coconut milk

500g tiny new
potatoes, halved

3/4 cup (150g) red lentils

1 tablespoon finely
chopped fresh coriander

Cut kumara into 3cm pieces.
Heat oil in large saucepan; cook onion, garlic,
ginger, sambal and spices, stirring, until
fragrant. Add sauce, peanut butter, stock,
coconut milk and potatoes; simmer, covered,
5 minutes. Add lentils and kumara; simmer,
covered, stirring often, about 20 minutes
or until vegetables are tender.
Serve sprinkled with fresh coriander.

SERVES 4
Per serving 37.3g fat; 3085kJ

lentil potato burgers

- ¹/₂ cup (100g) red lentils
- 2 tablespoons vegetable oil
- 2 medium sebago potatoes (400g), peeled, grated coarsely
- 1 medium brown onion (150g), chopped finely
- 1 clove garlic, crushed
- 1 teaspoon mild curry paste
- 1 teaspoon ground cumin
- 1 teaspoon garam masala
- 1 tablespoon finely chopped fresh mint
- ¹/₂ cup (75g) plain flour
- 1 egg, beaten lightly
- ¹/₂ cup (50g) packaged breadcrumbs
- 6 bread rolls
- 60g mesclun

mustard sauce

- ²/₃ cup (160g) sour cream
- 1 tablespoon seeded mustard
- 1 tablespoon finely chopped fresh chives
- 2 teaspoons finely chopped fresh mint

Cook lentils in medium saucepan of boiling water, uncovered, about 10 minutes or until tender; drain.

Meanwhile, heat oil in medium frying pan; cook potato, onion and garlic, stirring, until potato is soft. Add paste and spices; cook until fragrant.

Combine lentils and potato mixture in medium bowl; stir in mint, flour and egg. Cover; refrigerate 30 minutes. Using hands, shape mixture into six patties; coat in breadcrumbs.

Cook patties in heated oiled large frying pan until lightly browned on both sides.

Split rolls; toast. Top with patties, mesclun and mustard sauce.

Mustard Sauce Combine ingredients in small bowl.

SERVES 6
Per serving 20.9g fat; 2025kJ

60

glossary

bacon rashers also known as slices of bacon; made from cured, smoked pork side.

baking powder a raising agent consisting mainly of two parts cream of tartar to one part bicarbonate of soda (baking soda).

beef mince also known as ground beef.

breadcrumbs
packaged: fine-textured, crunchy, commercially purchased particles.
stale: one- or two-day-old bread made into crumbs by grating, blending or processing.

broad beans also known as fava beans; available fresh, canned and frozen. Best eaten having discarded both the long pod and the tough pale-green inner shell.

butter use salted or unsalted ("sweet") butter; 125g is equal to 1 stick butter.

buttermilk (1.8g fat per 100ml) sold with fresh milk products; despite the implication of its name, is low in fat.

capsicum also known as bell pepper or, simply, pepper. Discard membranes and seeds before use.

cheese
fetta: crumbly sheep-milk cheese with salty taste.
pizza: a commercial blend of varying proportions of processed grated cheddar, mozzarella and parmesan.
raclette: the generic name of a semi-hard cheese, gold in colour with small holes and a light brown rind. It has a distinct nutty flavour.

chicken mince finely ground fresh chicken.

chilli, thai red to dark-green in colour; small medium-to-hot chillies.

coconut milk pure, unsweetened coconut milk, available in cans.

cream (minimum fat content 35%) also known as pure cream and pouring cream; contains no additives.
light sour: (minimum fat content 18%) cultured to produce its characteristic tart flavour; thinner than normal sour cream.
sour: (minimum fat content 35%) a thick, commercially cultured soured cream.
thickened: (minimum fat content 35%) whipping cream; contains a thickener.

crème fraîche: (minimum fat content 35%) a fermented cream having a slightly tangy, nutty flavour and velvety rich texture.

flour
plain: all-purpose flour, made from wheat.
self-raising: plain flour sifted with baking powder in the proportion of 1 cup flour to 2 teaspoons baking powder.

garam masala a blend of roasted, ground spices, containing cardamom, clove, cinnamon, coriander, fennel and cumin.

ghee clarified butter, with the milk solids removed.

gherkin also known as a cornichon; young, dark-green cucumbers.

horseradish cream prepared paste of grated horseradish, vinegar, oil and sugar.

kumara Polynesian name of orange-fleshed sweet potato often confused with yam.

lamb
eye of loin: a cut derived from a row of loin chops. Once the bone and fat are removed, the larger portion is referred to as the eye of the loin.

lemon pepper seasoning a blend of crushed black pepper, lemon and spices.

mesclun a salad mix with a mixture of assorted young lettuce and other green leaves.

oil

cooking-oil spray: vegetable oil in an aerosol can, available in supermarkets.

olive: mono-unsaturated; made from the pressing of tree-ripened olives. Extra virgin and virgin are the highest quality olive oils, obtained from the first pressings of the olives. Extra light or light describes the milder flavours, not the fat levels.

peanut: pressed from ground peanuts; has high smoke point.

vegetable: any of a number of oils sourced from plants rather than animal fats.

onion

green: also known as scallion or (incorrectly) shallot; an immature onion picked before the bulb has formed, having a long, bright-green edible stalk.

red: also known as Spanish, red Spanish or Bermuda onion; a sweet-flavoured, large, purple-red onion. Good eaten raw in salads.

panch phora a combination of five aromatic seeds – cumin, fennel, mustard, fenugreek and kalonji (black onion) – fried in hot oil before being used in various meat and vegetable dishes.

pitta bread Lebanese wheat-flour bread.

pumpkin also known as squash; we used butternut pumpkin in these recipes unless specified otherwise.

rocket also known as arugula, rugula and rucola; a fresh, green, spicy salad leaf.

scallops a bivalve mollusc with fluted shell; the coral (roe) can be removed before use, if desired.

spinach correct name for this leafy green vegetable; often called English spinach or, incorrectly, silverbeet. A small, or "baby", variety is tender enough to be eaten raw in salads.

stock 1 cup (250ml) stock is the equivalent of 1 cup (250ml) water plus one crumbled stock cube (or 1 teaspoon stock powder).

sugar we used coarse granulated table sugar, also known as crystal sugar, unless otherwise specified.

brown: a soft, fine sugar retaining molasses.

caster: also known as superfine or finely granulated table sugar.

tikka paste Indian paste of chilli, coriander, cumin, garlic, ginger, turmeric, oil, fennel, pepper, cinnamon and cardamom.

tomato paste triple-concentrated tomato puree used as a flavouring.

vinegar

balsamic: authentic only from Modena, Italy; made from regional wine of white Trebbiano grapes then aged in antique casks.

yogurt we use unflavoured, full-fat yogurt unless stated otherwise.

worcestershire sauce thin, dark-brown spicy sauce used both as a seasoning and as a condiment.

MEASURES

One Australian metric measuring cup holds approximately 250ml, one Australian metric tablespoon holds 20ml, one Australian metric teaspoon holds 5ml.

The difference between one country's measuring cups and another's is within a 2- or 3-teaspoon variance, and will not affect your cooking results. North America, New Zealand and the United Kingdom use a 15ml tablespoon. All cup and spoon measurements are level. The most accurate way of measuring dry ingredients is to weigh them. When measuring liquids, use a clear glass or plastic jug with metric markings.

We use large eggs with an average weight of 60g.

DRY MEASURES

METRIC	IMPERIAL
15g	½oz
30g	1oz
60g	2oz
90g	3oz
125g	4oz (¼lb)
155g	5oz
185g	6oz
220g	7oz
250g	8oz (½lb)
280g	9oz
315g	10oz
345g	11oz
375g	12oz (¾lb)
410g	13oz
440g	14oz
470g	15oz
500g	16oz (1lb)
750g	24oz (1½lb)
1kg	32oz (2lb)

LIQUID MEASURES

METRIC	IMPERIAL
30ml	1 fluid oz
60ml	2 fluid oz
100ml	3 fluid oz
125ml	4 fluid oz
150ml	5 fluid oz (¼ pint/1 gill)
190ml	6 fluid oz
250ml	8 fluid oz
300ml	10 fluid oz (½ pint)
500ml	16 fluid oz
600ml	20 fluid oz (1 pint)
1000ml (1 litre)	1¾ pints

LENGTH MEASURES

METRIC	IMPERIAL
3mm	⅛in
6mm	¼in
1cm	½in
2cm	¾in
2.5cm	1in
5cm	2in
6cm	2½in
8cm	3in
10cm	4in
13cm	5in
15cm	6in
18cm	7in
20cm	8in
23cm	9in
25cm	10in
28cm	11in
30cm	12in (1ft)

OVEN TEMPERATURES

These oven temperatures are only a guide for conventional ovens.
For fan-forced ovens, check the manufacturer's manual.

	°C (CELSIUS)	°F (FAHRENHEIT)	GAS MARK
Very slow	120	250	½
Slow	150	275 – 300	1 – 2
Moderately slow	160	325	3
Moderate	180	350 – 375	4 – 5
Moderately hot	200	400	6
Hot	220	425 – 450	7 – 8
Very hot	240	475	9

index

63

Are you missing some of the world's favourite cookbooks?

The Australian Women's Weekly cookbooks are available from bookshops, cookshops, supermarkets and other stores all over the world. You can also buy direct from the publisher, using the order form below.

MINI SERIES £3.50 190x138MM 64 PAGES

TITLE	QTY	TITLE	QTY	TITLE	QTY
4 Fast Ingredients		Grills & Barbecues		Quick Desserts	
4 Kids to Cook		Healthy Everyday Food 4 Kids		Roast	
15-minute Feasts		Ice-creams & Sorbets		Salads	
50 Fast Chicken Fillets		Indian Cooking		Simple Slices	
50 Fast Desserts		Indonesian Favourite		Simply Seafood	
Barbecue Chicken		Irish Favourites		Soup plus	
Biscuits, Brownies & Bisottti		Italian Favourites		Spanish Favourites	
Bites		Jams & Jellies		Stir-fries	
Bowl Food		Japanese Favourites		Stir-fry Favourites	
Burgers, Rösti & Fritters		Kebabs & Skewers		Summer Salads	
Cafe Cakes		Kids Party Food		Tagines & Couscous	
Cafe Food		Lebanese Cooking		Tapas, Antipasto & Mezze	
Casseroles & Curries		Low-Fat Delicious		Tarts	
Char-grills & Barbecues		Low Fat Fast		Tex-Mex	
Cheesecakes, Pavlova & Trifles		Malaysian Favourites		Thai Favourites	
Chinese Favourites		Mince Favourites		The Fast Egg	
Chocolate Cakes		Microwave		The Young Chef	
Crumbles & Bakes		Muffins		Vegetarian	
Cupcakes & Cookies		Noodles & Stir-fries		Vegie Main Meals	
Dips & Dippers		Old-Fashioned Desserts		Vietnamese Favourites	
Dried Fruit & Nuts		Outdoor Eating		Wok	
Drinks		Packed Lunch			
Easy Pies & Pastries		Party Food			
Fast Fillets		Pickles and Chutneys			
Fishcakes & Crispybakes		Pasta			
Gluten-free Cooking		Potatoes		TOTAL COST £	

Photocopy and complete coupon below

Name _____

Address _____

_____ Postcode _____

Country _____ Phone (business hours) _____

Email*(optional) _____
* By including your email address, you consent to receipt of any email regarding this magazine, and other emails which inform you of ACP's other publications, products, services and events, and to promote third party goods and services you interested in.

I enclose my cheque/money order for £ _____ or please charge £ _____ to m

☐ Access ☐ Mastercard ☐ Visa ☐ Diners Club

Card number | | | | | | | | | | | | | | | |

3 digit security code *(found on reverse of card)* _____

Cardholder's signature _____ Expiry date ____

To order: Mail or fax – photocopy or complete the order form above, and send your credit card details or cheque payable to: Australian Consolidated Press (UK), 10 Scirocco Close, Moulton Park Office Northampton NN3 6AP, phone (+44) (01) 604 642200, fax (+44) (01) 604 642300, e-mail books@acpu or order online at www.acpuk.com
Non-UK residents: We accept the credit cards listed on the coupon, or cheques, drafts or International M Orders payable in sterling and drawn on a UK bank. Credit card charges are at the exchange rate currer time of payment. All pricing current at time of going to press and subject to change/availability.
Postage and packing UK: Add £1.00 per order plus 75p per book.
Postage and packing overseas: Add £2.00 per order plus £1.50 per book. **Offer ends 31.12.2009**